AF776653

WHAT CAME DOWN IN THE SMOKE

WHAT CAME DOWN

IN THE SMOKE

SUMMER J. HART

JACKLEG PRESS

jacklegpress.org
summerjhart.com

Published by JackLeg Press 2026.
©2026 Summer Hart.
All rights reserved.
Printed in the United States of America.

ISBN: 978-1956907988

No part of this work may be reproduced or publicized in any form or by any means, electronic or mechanical, including photocopying, microfilm, recording, or by any information storage and retrieval system, without permission in writing from the publisher. However, authors maintain ownership rights of their individual poems, and as such retain all rights to publish and republish their work.

Library of Congress Control Number: 2025942872

Cover art: Turkey buzzard: Cathartes aura. Male, 1. Young, 2. c.1 v.2 plate 151, Vultures, Turkey vulture. From the original prints by John James Audubon, *Birds of America*.
Credit: piemags/DMC/Alamy.

PRAISE

To map by grief a path between two points lacks the vision Summer J. Hart shares in these tender, grit-held poems that stand as testament to the multitude of points and paths one must chart in this life. These poems seek to know and teach survival in a world wracked with violence. How do we move through grief? Through the pieces we break down into and reassemble, that we summon through language, memory, and attending to the continued act of being. Through the coexistence of memory, the daily banal, and small celebrations, small acts of attention, what is offered is not resolution, but perhaps a persistent attention to *being* as a state and verb, a point and a path always still becoming.
—Abigail Chabitnoy, author of *In the Current Where Drowning is Beautiful*

Moving through prose poems and lyric narratives, Summer J. Hart's collection splits story open to examine what animates it, drawing the reader into a forward drift through loss and return. These poems assemble meaning through a luminous accretion of sharp instances—jagged in texture, electric with juxtaposition. Drawing on myth and inherited story, the work recalls the moment in "IN THE STORY 'SURVIVAL' BY RITA JOE" when a baby returns to life after suckling a beaver's tail, a reminder that the rituals of living are not meant to preserve life but sustain it.

Threaded with charged negative space, the poems hold the dead and the living in uneasy coexistence. "Dear Violet, I was thinking. Of teeth & skulls & stones. Of being a witch or fisherwoman or poet." Part field study, part record of daily life, this book sustains a radiant

simultaneity—an aurora only Hart can see—where meaning gathers in what refuses to disappear.
—Diana Marie Delgado, author of *Tracing the Horse*

Summer J. Hart's newest book pulses with life, its vivacity made more exhilarating and exquisite by how poised the poems are, too, on the brink of pain, loss, grief, vulnerability, and death. Correlatively, Hart's poetic voice throughout the book is—somehow, miraculously, all at once—as clamorous and insistent as the cry of a Valkyrie and as aching and tender as a nightingale's. Her turns of phrase are so surprising and fresh that one feels constantly, as one moves from line to line and page to page, as though one has stumbled on a scene of intimacy—two lovers furtively kissing or a mother nursing a tiny child to sleep—that does not belong to one, but an intimacy that one is allowed to witness, nonetheless.
—Eleanor Johnson, author of *Scream with Me: Horror Films and the Rise of American Feminism*

What Came down in the Smoke is a book of gorgeous lines for catching the uncatchable—what burns, or rots, or disintegrates in the fog at the edge of a field. Hart's sensibility hangs at the mycelial edge of abundance, where lushness tips with creative energy, transforming but never forgetting the embodied histories it holds. These poems will feed you fiddleheads, cheap wine, snakeskins, "how scientists found a bacterium that can eat time," and their capacity for noticing is never less than electric.
—Laura Marris, Author of *The Age of Loneliness*

Summer J. Hart is a revelation. *What Came Down in the Smoke* is a lucid and lyrical account of family and its secrets, love and its losses. These are poems that will steal your breath and stay in your mind.
—Anahid Nersessian, author of *Keats's Odes: A Lover's Discourse*

Summer J. Hart is a canny magician, seeming to direct the reader's eye toward the macabre, then teasing these images apart with a sculptor's care for the pause, the space, the precisely chosen word that redirects the narrative toward beauty and magic and survival. Exquisitely wrought prose blocks mingle with stacked poems, lines that break and reform on the page. A quirky cast of characters suggests memory fragments in a swirling mosaic of images that catch the light and shimmer with the sly humor of a Wabanaki story well told.
—Diane Wilson, author of *The Seed Keeper*

CONTENTS

for Matt

BONE HOLD

A pair of eagles nest in the fork of a snag.

Albumen, yolk-sac, embryo. Perched just above the

            river.

My sister & I snap the garden's shells. We load sweet green

            ammunition into our mouths.

. . .

Never eat the liver. Or kidneys. Of a moose. Remember.

Remember to bury the

                        heart.

Toss the bones in the bone hold.

            Everyone knows the rubbish of animals goes in

            a woods grave.

. . .

Dearly Departed Laundry Detergent, Liquor Bottles,

Rib, Haunch,

            We have gathered here 12 femurs, 18 jaws.

            Some waste is laced with cadmium, mercury.

            Some, fluorine & carbon.

. . .

Red patrols his garden with a shotgun & a lot of DDT.

The ghost of a crow perches on the stake

                    its body is wired to.

I watch it
          watching,

watching me.

A moth flies out of its eye socket.

Yellow & black striped beetles

          collapse

                    into dust.

. . .

Dear Darlings, forever & Today,

          Deliver us our Daily milk Through Aqueous Film

          Forming Foam & silt.

          with love, your lifetime health advisory.

. . .

Red pays us to pick off the potato beetles.

Winnie brings us orange slices.

We drain the fruit like Bunnicula.

Juice runs down the corners of my sister's mouth.

I smile behind pulp like a boxer.

…

Our fingers
unearth
potatoes

purple like
Easter.

Brush soil

from tender
red skin,

put the worms
back in.

A surprise
blue one! We
eat it

with butter
& buckshot.

Plink in the
sink, plink.

Plink. Pink

around the
wound

yellow with
cream,

runner & wax
bean.

You’re mince-
meat when I
catch you.

No, you are.

…

You can strip layers back. Turn the earth. You won't retrieve it. It travels networks of mycelium. Over the backs of rivers. Through worms. You. Won't. It slides from stomach to stomach. What was once the slick of a microwave popcorn bag is now organ. Meat.

The cat swats a crisp dead fly off the windowsill.

Chicken & shell. The words we eat are too long to spell.

. . .

Dear Sweet Nugget,

I wanted to tell you that an owl's pellet

is a compression

of fur & bone.

Smaller than a mouse's skull, you are

not a milestone.

Not this little knot

of mine.

Not nothing.

But not plum. Not

avocado.

. . .

The crow's hoard no longer resembles fruit.

Mourning doves lift all at once.

Exchange bodies for weather.

. . .

Dear Sweet Nugget,

I only remember fragments. The blue infant bathtub

we bought off Craigslist. Tide pools of periwinkles &

whelks.

Rust-colored algae, pink sea stars.

Your father sobbing in the bathroom of the vacation

house

while I navigate a set of weather-rucked steps down to

the sea.

I must have tossed salt over the wrong shoulder.

Misunderstood & buried a nickel in someone else's

garden.

. . .

Soft-shell clam, belly full of sand, how'd you get to be so yummy?

Open up! Open up! Show me your tummy.

. . .

We dress the dogs in safety orange & take go-wine to the gravel pit. I learn that the deer here are contaminated. That chemicals passed from mill sludge to river to grass to doe to fawn in utero & will never go away. The state of Maine announces a Do-Not-Eat Advisory over Thanksgiving. Bodies are left to carrion birds & coyotes. But we already knew. Not to. Do not. Eat. The liver.

No more than one per year.

Remember.

…

Dear Sweet Nugget,

Pink beach roses grow in thickets over orange lichen

covered rock.

We knew it would happen, but not when.

We didn't think it would be like *this*, sunlight on

serpentine. Matt driving

too fast.   Me, folded on a pink & white striped towel.

A fawn running along the causeway.

The only way I can describe it is,

the dog caught her ear & it won't stop bleeding.

…

To draw the grit out, add one rusted nail & soak overnight in a bean pot. Lay a red & white checkered cloth over the picnic table.

Pin the corners with four granite stones.

Place a fork to the left of each plate.

Knife & spoon go on the right.

No plastic cutlery. No lazy picnic-ware.   Candle in a hurricane.

…

We dig clams. Cook them with sea beans

& butter.

Our jaws don't lock lucky, lucky ducks.

I peel away the gray film. Reveal a glistening neck.

…

Oh, Darlin',

Don't be so hard

so hard on yourself

don't be so hard

your face is going to stick like that.

…

We eat handfuls of mud
cake.

Pour more
& more

cheap red
wine.

…

I walk outside. Stumble barefoot across salted grass. Wade into the receding tide in a rush of jasper & glass. The trick is to go numb. When you can't feel your ankles, go in up to your knees. Up to your hips. Collarbones. To your eyes. *Go ahead.* All the way under.

…

One part of this story is August 17, 2008, Deer Isle, Maine.

Another part is earlier. On a rectangular garden plot overlooking the Penobscot River, dusted & fortified. Tall & green in summer. Brown in November. Black-winged bodies shot from the sky are nailed to iron posts. Wooden posts. Hung from wires. No, twine. Memory is to garden as garden is to mortuary. At dawn, a moose passes through. I collect nails from the yard in a coffee can. The three-legged dog howls, jowl-deep in Pink Panther. I sit by a white peony watching ants line up for nectar. When it's time for supper,

I don't go in.

. . .

The thing is. Some dirt eats & eats. Some dirt is starving.

The thing is. You were & weren't ever mine, Darling Clementine.

The thing is. I'll never really know.

. . .

I told one lie. I didn't find you like a speckled bean in the grass.

What I found were snakes in the myrtle.

. . .

You would have been 18 this February.

My sister shows me a deer skull with a hole instead of antlers.

We compare scars. Tattoos.

I show her the small wild violet on my wrist.

Tell her how scientists found a bacterium that can eat time.

>>

THE SUMMER I TURN 33 & ASK TIM TO SHAVE MY HEAD

27 vultures kettle above the manor house lawn.

I laugh because
          the yoga teacher

posts the video from her outdoor class with the caption:

I could just lay here all day in Shavasana, watching these graceful hawks…

But it's not *really* funny.   Out here they'll peck a calf to death.

          Out here you must
                    remember to turn your sheep.

I count three dead woolly bears, one mantis, one sparrow.

The night after I receive the bad news, my parents sleep on our
          couch. Matt & I stay

          out,   stuff ourselves silly with meat & gin.

We go carrion, carnivore /   stumble through the back gate /
                    squalling like bobcats.

I bite until skin breaks. He pulls up clods with earthworms dangling

          & hurls
                    them at the fence.

          We fuck in the shade garden, on ostrich ferns & pink-

blossomed variegated hostas.

Fuck. Fuck. Fuck.

Back into loam.

IN THE STORY "SURVIVAL" BY RITA JOE

Parents sacrifice their child to the snow.

Dress her in skins tanned with liver & brain.

Such is the logic of dying.

If our baby freezes to death,
we'll survive by eating her flesh.

Weeping, she's loosed through a hole in the roof.

Near dawn, the wind still a-howlin'
through the hole, the dead girl

comes crawlin'

blood on blue

lips
an unnatural
hue

from suckling

a frozen beaver's tail.

THE SMALLER THE ANIMAL THE LARGER THE HEART

The boy is crying in bed. Matt & I take down the scrub maple & plant a blue spruce & a redbud. Our apple tree is blossoming. The neighbors' kid is building a dirt bike jump that looks like a Scooby Doo death trap. It's an ugly thought, but I want him to break something. The cat leaves a gift under the coffee table. Still, soft / still soft & gray. *I'll put you to bed with cotton & thread. A walnut for your cradle.* The thing is, I found it, so the mouse ghost belongs to me. That's just how it goes. Other things I've found in this carpet:

pennies, shards of glass, shards of bone, cat claws, river stones, wine stains, curry stains & a milk tooth. Last summer, the boy & the neighbors' kid dug a trench & filled it with water. They built a fort with old windows & scraps of pressure-treated lumber. The cat stalks a Japanese lady beetle across the window seat. Rubs her head against the dog's bad eye. *You are one of the things that I eat, first you are warmth & then you are meat.* I offer Buffy & double dark chocolate chunk cookies. The boy won't come out. Won't let me in.

FALSE SPRING

I untangle
the horse's
mane with
my fingers,
dab

ointment
to its rain-
rotted
crest.
Two men

coax
an auger
from a long,
thin box.
Wary-

eyed dogs
bark
through
Shrinky
Dinked

windows.
The drug
store on
the corner
is over-

stuffed.
We wait
fifteen
minutes
in folding

chairs.
Baby-darling,
Dearest,
My Dear,
croon

the fiber-
optic hearts
of half-
price love-
sick bears.

SEA SMOKE, FLASHLIGHT FROZEN TO A MITTEN

To new beginnings then.

I burn dead wood
in a coffee can.

The Barolo we were saving has turned
to vinegar.

I smudge.

Cedar.
Turkey feather.

Abalone.

I write to the poet with the
sparklers

my parents brought last July.

Go in.

Flip the record.

Bob my head to The Barrel.

Go out.

Smudge again.

The night smells of sulfur,
twine,

singed leaves,
rotten wine.

PINK MOON

Pink as the crescent of rose quartz you gave me that fits to my thumb perfectly, like my thumb fits inside your body. Your body, the tub, the quartz, my thumb. A bottle of pink wine left in the sun. I find a wishing stone with a forked band of lightning. Split like the lifeline in my palm. I watch from the audience. You perform in front of a life-sized photograph of a woman, black & white, & you, also black & white, split from the photo as if by trick of the light. It's time to get up. No. *It's the poet.* I forget I'm sleeping. Last night, the rain came sideways. The verge is a colony of snails.

LET US CONTINUE THIS FLAVORFUL JOURNEY

Behind the chain-link fence,

coyotes watch

the naturalist
secure
the body.
Thin
as
spent
grass.

The Old Timer tells us to look to the north

side of the largest
tree
for drops.

I swear I saw a golden eagle, I text my sister, *on the Palisades.*

Daffodils & alliums are early, despite the chickadees' prediction.

I find turkey tail under the snow.

Do you remember that restaurant with talking taxidermy?

Do you remember the summer we saved those frogs?

It's her birthday.

The dog passes a kidney stone.

She refuses to kiss the moose.

LOVE LETTER

I love the gray fox hidden in the meadow that used to hide deer & before that was a battery factory, but the soil is fine now. Still, we don't dare eat the river grapes. I love knocking the first shed out of the curry comb against Barb's tack box. *Thwuck! Thwuck!* I love you, not because you kicked a pokeweed, but that you know to call me

when our dog walker startles a vulture off the lawn. You know it will fill me with delight to hear how the vulture takes flight with the squirrel it is rending. *Keep your dog inside a while.* Here is where anecdote becomes love letter. The moment the bird drops its heart.

TOO MANY QUEENS & THE CATTLE GO TATTY

When the clams die off, we'll eat the lawn—

purslane, dandelion.

The meadow is a buzzing picnic spread.

        Rosehip & goldthread

are old medicine.

        Bumblebee in anemone.

We'll need something

to chew between meals,   pine needles or
        spruce pitch.

        Hey!

                A little brown bat & a barred owl

                are warming
                        themselves by the fire.

                My sister's dog gets loose & takes a chicken.

                        Resin fills up the heart.

                Her apple tree,
                        girdled by mice.

SOMEONE DIES EVERY YEAR THINKING THEY FOUND A WILD CARROT

Another well goes offline. My therapist says it's developmentally appropriate to feel as if I am running out of time. When Mom & my sister deliver Christmas presents to Winnie, they find her in bed. Unmoving. Blackened potato in the oven. Front door open. Purse on the kitchen table. She dies a week later from leukemia. No one knew until she started bleeding. Strawberry windchime. Pewter thimble. Chipped porcelain teacup. I don't make it up for her funeral. I don't get to make it up to her. The woodstove. Red's lobster trap coffee table. The plastic lobsters. Date cookies, forget-me-not saucer. Nadine doesn't go because she has a cat & a dog & a kennel full of cats & dogs. The antique doll in Winnie's bedroom blinks its one good eye. The virus in my mouth tastes like copper.

. . .

The boy tells me he ate a wild carrot at summer camp. The secret is to dig it out of the meadow before it blooms. *If it smells like a carrot*, the counselor warned, *it's already too late*. How to tell without umbel, bee's nest, garland? Before the queen pricks her finger.

. . .

It's 4:30 & already pitch dark. I'm making a Christmas ornament for Winnie out of an acorn & a walnut shell. I cut mouse ears from gray felt & glue them to the acorn's cap. I pull apart a cotton ball. Cover each half with fabric. One for her bonnet. One for her quilt.

I READ SOMEWHERE

a married woman is a plague of locusts.

Such destruction /   Oh, such havoc /
            Her lips on yours

a decimated field,
a chemical stirring,
lace cut by ancient bodies.

The cows starve,
the people starve,
shouting won't dislodge her.

LAST YEAR'S SMOKE

Gossamer webs in yew

catch dew

        that smells
like pinecones burning.

Red sun morning / red sun,
        in mourning.

Our neighbor declares

        the cardinals are at war
                with the crows

                again.

                I saw you feeding them.

                        She sweeps

                                        tiny bones

                        into the lavender.

MOTHERFUCKING SNAKES

On the flight home
I read the poet's novel

about poets
fucking & going

mad. I can still feel
the heat of her.

Dear little tongue, red as grenadine.
Sugar in your teacup, soot in your cream.

This is the sound of a snake shedding its

skin.

Night after night,
ringing its lover's

doorbell.

Mother-
fucking
snakes.

When the two sisters accidentally marry stars—

That's when I cry.

Bodies burning through sky.
I lift the forbidden rock.

Peer down at the sidewalk.
Take in the stomped husks

of lanternflies,

shattered
wind-

shield,
a penny,

luck-
side

down.

THERE'S SOMETHING IRREGULAR ABOUT THIS RAIN

Before Powwow,

I trim the boy's hair.

Leave dead ends

        in a cup on the windowsill.

        Moonlight. For growing. Pinch of tobacco.

Don't worry.

                What's she called again? Hazel eyes. No.

Violet.

                All hair & belly.

It goes like this every day. One child's name & then the next.

Show me your beautiful braids. No.   Tell me something.

        Beautiful.

Please remember. Please. Don't.

        Tell me.

        The boy finds two balloons behind the couch.

Gold, then white.

The cat brings in a mouse.

The cat brings in a pigeon.

The cat brings in a duck.

In the city, magpies build nests with anti-bird spikes,

candy wrappers, cigarette butts.

Artificial air

for artificial breath.

Artificial thorns

for artificial nests.

[blows / please don't choke / blows again]

Did Violet go in the water? I can't see her anymore.

It's starting to rain.   Again.

Shhhh.

Pinch of salt. Pat of butter. Eat around the bones.

The news comes during The Grand Entry.

Comes in on hunter's

feet.

Comes in with its head

dangling.

What the news is, I don't yet know.

The boy sits in the mud outside the tent.

Blue smoke

pours up

from the
stacks

across the river.

TONIGHT, I'M HOT FOR YOU

Because you wrote a poem. Kicked that pokeweed.
          Grew some dill.

HOW TO PREVENT A HOUSE FIRE

Wind cords around lamps. Pull furniture away from walls. Cry just thinking about what could have happened. Unplug.   Coffee pot.

Unplug.   Washing machine. Unplug.

Phone.   *Is anyone here?*

Touch ever so lightly.

Hover your fingers, really, over the planchette.

In my dream, I nudge the shrimp-curved body of a cicada killer through a crack in the floor. At the barn, I find a drowned mouse in each water bucket. How to trust anything these days? No one is safe from curses or thirst. How to trust with all these spirits. Dead men left in maple sugar camps, witches with fireball eyes, lovers who are stars or snakes during the day. I read about rivers of fire

that burn secretly. Underground.

For years.

Pssiip!   Vinyl siding bursts over the too-close grill.

Fsssss . . . That's the wedding album

melting into carpet that's melting

into

linoleum.   Sometimes the microwave runs all night,

Sally says. You must unplug

it. In case of a power surge.   Electrical storm.

Cigarette butt.   Dead squirrel.

Curling

iron
left

in

the sink.

If his eyes become swirling infernos, the only solution

is to burn it all down. It was a ball of lightning.
Came through the phone line. The Pipes.

The bathtub.

Authorities say they found fresh

blood on the mouth of the corpse & the one

hanging in the tree was also well fed.

These are just stories.

Please touch me.

Where?

I point to the red dot on the screen that marks the animal I've been researching newly extinct.

Rosy-red as a shined apple's cheek.

Mark *me.*

My skin, my flesh, my poison pips.

I DIDN'T MY BEST

The mark is the result of what I pretended to draw. It's the consequence. Ink bleeding through paper. Through faux grain presswood. Mark as memory. Memory-skin. Like how beetle kill pine is a blue reaction. Residue. The technician points to the dot on the screen. A blue-black pip / fuzzed. In ink-terms, its edges are *feathered.* She uses the words *ill-defined* & *occlusion.* When we were kids, my sister liked to eat wild apples, core & all. I warned her about things that take root. That accumulate.

We climb to the top of the tree. Cut out the worms. She chews the skin, flesh & seeds. The paper is snow-blind white. I tear it in half. Peel away the top layer like I peeled the sunburn I got when Matt & I visited my grandparents in Vero Beach. Back then everyone was still alive & we got along by not talking politics. I saw a shark that day & two manatees.   The paper holds onto the mark the way wood holds memory.   Of being.

Buck. Chip. Pulp. Wash. Finish.

I comfort this body.

Matt brings me a blanket
& a knit hat.

Rubs the wax off an apple.

Knock, knock. Who's there?

As instructed, I draw two dots on either end

of a fresh sheet of paper.

I use my grief to map the path between them.

That was a lie.

I don't follow the poet's instructions.

Instead, I stamp two circles in the snow but leave them unconnected. Ice melts off the roof & pools on the deck. The fire pit is heaped with wet ash & weeds. Stain chips off the Adirondack chairs.

One • is the house. The other • is the falling-down shed. One • is the rotten dogwood & the other • is a grass green pinecone. One • is the porch swing we don't take down for winter & the other • is six more • s. One • for each forgotten watermelon in the garden. One • is the very good dog & the other • is a well of yellow-orange dog urine. One • is the neighbor who tells us the soil tested positive for lead & *do not to eat those wine caps fruiting under the fence.* The other • is a wasp in the yew. One • is the antique cobalt blue bottle we find while digging post holes. The other • is a vulture's feather. One • is a slash of pink in the sky. The other • is the ghost of a doe

[breathe, this

is an

intermission]

& her twin ghost fawns are two • s. One • is the rust-brown water that comes out of the tap in October. The other • is the crabgrass & mare's tail Matt yanks from the lawn. One • is the neighbors' cat peering out of the window. The other • is my cat, buried next to the chimney. One • is the pea-sized density I find in my left breast & the other • marks its position on my skin. One • is the mostly empty bottle of Ativan sitting on my nightstand. The other • is a four-leaf clover I find in the park. One • is a clump of black earth tongues. Dad texts, *Don't eat those.* The other • is a crow tearing a hole in a black plastic bag. One • is the shadow on my lung that turns out to be nothing. The other • is the shadow over my heart that turns out to be something.

THE GOOD NEWS

The summers the boy was five & six
        & a masterful yard sale negotiator,

he amassed a collection of porcelain
        dolls that traveled everywhere with us

buckled in the backseat—the boy, his
        dolls, their asynchronous winking eyes.

/

He called them The Doll Land Army.
        I sewed green uniforms with toothpick

swords & Matt built them a fort
        in the woods behind my parents' house.

//

The boy didn't mean to break them—
        nevertheless, one by one they succumbed

to mortal injury & with great ceremony
        the boy buried them in the garden

by the stone wall with the climbing
        wild roses. My mother watched while

collecting the hips. *Don't worry, Grammie,*
        the boy grinned, *they'll rise again in the spring.*

///

Winter comes quick after pickling season.
        My mother tied back stalks to decompose,

bulbs asleep under earth rigid
        & sparkling. Garden erased by weather.

////

After the melt,
        my mother called with the good news.

Row after row, chipped faces pushed
        through soil dotted with crocus & snow

drop, cheeks still blushing, brown &
        gold ringlets matted, eyes unblinking

through plastic wrap. The boy's fallen
        battalion resurrected by frost heave.

MILLIPEDE SEASON

I make a study of the raven.

Ruff,
belly,
crum-

bled
on the
side-

walk
on,
dog.

Walk on. I'm not ready to go.

Shadow by shadow, collected.

The artist assembles a dead raven from strips of discarded tire. It's almost. The same thing, I guess. Hackled. Bent. In the photograph the lapsed poet sends, four vultures bathe in a creek. One of them pins the remains of an opossum to a rock. In the photograph I send her, fourteen vultures are gathered on the lawn of the medical center, tugging rot from the grass. Matt picks up beetle-blued wood & I think about bodies that stain, fruit; about the little cup of mountain laurel the lapsed poet stuck to her t-shirt; about *the symmetry of cows, birthed in fields of fresh-calved fieldstone.* It's millipede season. I count twelve live, eight dead. The dog's slowing down.

All of us, slowing.

WHAT CAME DOWN IN THE SMOKE

Poetry is our medium.

At the dead center of us, she wrote.

My beloved.

I bring you.   Gifts.

Sudden agitation of butterflies.

          Aphids cloud the swimming pool.

My
husband
knows

but her
wife does
not.

A dark
& twist-
ing plot,

this book
about
burning.

BEFORE THE RUPTURE

I get new nipples
from Vinny

in Baltimore because the ones

the surgeon
made from my thigh

black-
ened

& fell

in the
shower.

Still.

Still. I dream of nursing—

no

not

of

starting
over.

. . .

I ease the tick out of my hip, leaving mouth

& palp intact.

Nothing left behind.

embedded.

…

I'm sitting on the bed

undressed from the waist down.

That's how Matt finds me.

He takes the tweezers from my hand.

I tell him to crush the body. Set it on fire.

To end something properly, you must macerate. Burn.

…

Vinny says my inks are dark honey & warm mink.

He tells me about his hamster blanket.

How he hand-stitched it from 300 pelts.

I keep very still.

Through the window,

I watch a pileated

woodpecker

hammer at a stump.

…

I'm undressed from the waist up.

White sneakers

squeak on

gray linoleum

or maybe that color is psychology blue.

The surgeon directs me to pull down my pants.

She slaps my thighs, dissatisfied.

You don't have enough of a fat blanket.

. . .

It's so soft, Vinny's blanket.

The blanket with 600 eyes.

Thock! Thock! Thock!

Goes the downward

planar arc

of the bird's

red crest.

IN MY DREAM OF DEAD WASPS

I am physically fine, the poet says.

It must have been all that cow tongue she ate as a child.

She lights the end of a rolled-up newspaper.

THE MYTH ABOUT THE BEAR

When the bear

folded

neatly
behind
a rock

astral
projects

collects
winter-

berries
birch

fungus
willow
bark.

When the gentle-

man
with
rabbit's
feet

trades

his
grand-
mother

for an otter's pelt.

To France!

To France!

When a wolverine

freezes

snout
to lake

fresh

out of spells

out of matches

out of sticks

out of ashes—

I pick up my phone.

You haven't written.

I take a deep breath.

This time you won't.

CO-EXECUTORS OF THE WILL

The boy cups the translucent baby bluebird. He pushes it back through the little hole in the little bluebird box. When I tell Mom, she screams. I console. Scold. Put on a brave face. Matt cries alone in his office. I cry alone on the air mattress. Rage, in the car, between tests. I find a four-leaf clover.   So, it's true.

I've finally angered you out of love with me.

...

Palm through plate
glass.

My baby won't
latch.

This wig has a real
gray
hair.

...

Hello?

Hello?

Hello?

...

When Dad calls, I'm eating one half of the English cucumber I panic bought from the deli before my artist talk. I take another loop around the pond. *The poet wrote me for the last time while I was driving here*, I text. Alison calls this "transit news." Mom says the Mike Lewis painting goes to my sister. I get the naked ladies on the striped tablecloth one. Two bunches of bananas. An apple. Tipped-over wine glass. Women the size of green peppers. How did we get here? I pick up Matt's phone. Type, *What about my wife?*

. . .

Here we go again.

Remove the handset from the cradle.

Morning sun streams in through the window. Remove the handset.

From cradle.

Remove handset /
the cradle.

[softly] *Hello? I'm so —*

[louder] *No.*

. . .

Ms.? Tra LaLa

Ms.? Tra LaLa

Ms.? Tra LaLaLaLa LaLa La La

. . .

Bluebird prediction [sound happy]: *Can't get a red bird, jay bird'll do. I'll get another girl sweeter than you.* Mud season has begun. I visit two studios then follow the puddled road back to the meadow where I found the dead bee & write a poem about finding a dead bee. I tease up my bangs. *Claw me, baby.* Microwave apple & cinnamon flavored instant oatmeal. Eat it with a fork. Boombox prediction:

Leos, wear orange for a lucky Monday.

PRIEST & A PARCEL OF LAND

Nuthatches swarm the feeder.

The river has burst its banks.

A spotted turtle circles in a glass tank.

Over the river, I see an eagle, then the statue of an eagle. In the other river, fish boil. There's no place to hide in the other river. Brownish green. Yellowy pearl. Bait fish float on the surface. Pool. Still as. Heron. Mussel shells open. Scales drop into silt. Here an umbrella. Here tourists bathe. Here the basin widens, goes sandy.

A change in material property.

...

A burned-out priest gives a sermon in the burnt-out cathedral.

In my dream, swifts discover 3,200 unmarked graves.

Sally points to a stone wall at the edge of the property.

Somewhere over there, I think.

THE SKY'S GOT ITS NOSE OUT OF JOINT

Every time the clouds spit, the dog leans further into the
bathmat.

Plastic bats twirl in the neighbor's eaves.

A jumbo tarantula flashes red eyes through polyester webbing.

I watch a
woman
sweep the street with a metal detector.

I'm thinking about the way you said it: *Affair.*

Affair. Affair. Affair.

& how we are but also can't have one.

I use the language of [ ]

so I don't have to say [ ] or [ ] or I'm a [ ] & a [ ].

I never told you this, but when we were in New York

I recognized your dress from your engagement
photos.

I would write to you but my nose.

I would write to you but Trick! I would write to you but have
you checked the storm drain.

DEAR VIOLET

I was
thinking.

Perhaps,

if I
properly

cast.

The teeth from that opossum jaw.

Or

the bird skull

tucked in the nest made from

horsehair & lollipop

wrappers.

Or

one of the rounds of jasper

from the jar filled with sea glass &

marbles—

I know.

Let's make a game of it.

We'll skip across the water like stones.

I'll toss

& you'll come singing back with the
tide.

Or

I'll use a long steady line—

If I cast it

with precision,

I can reel you back to me, one crank at a
time.

Steady. Steady now. Little Spoon.

Darling Spinner.

As foretold by the bones or
stones or teeth or the line,

I will hold you for the first
time. My Bauble.   My Eye.

In your hospital hat

& fur-lined moccasins.

Dear Violet,

In those final hours, I wanted to feel our breaths catch in the brambles—to collect like dew at the nearest spindle-knot of a spider's web. Yes, I wanted this poem to smack of romance. Why else use words like *spindle-knot, dew*? I wanted to be moon & capillary, molecule & gravity, to control the movement of water like starlings & certain laws of the heart—& for you, My Dot, to be the speck of dirt inside each rain drop.

Dear Violet,

I was thinking. Of teeth & skulls & stones. Of being a witch or fisherwoman or poet. Of nevertheless losing you first in a towel & later to a dark tile floor & how you won't live on in the rain & how trite it is to say in the heart. I was thinking this as the air pimpled my arms wrapped around my rose-pricked knees & mosquitos, in the heat of mothering, tucked in. How easily I killed them. How the tide swelled pink & bulbous.

Dear Violet,

I climbed the
embankment,

back up
to your
father.

salt-
grass,

granite,

stone
wall,

beach roses, heavy with pollen.

Predict-
ably, I was pricked.

Arguably,
I was

un-
prepared

for this display of love

bloused

in every

sex—

stamens
erect,

pistils

quiver-
ing.

In the rose-
gold

of another sun-
set

I stood in that
thicket

dead-
heading

those fucking flowers.

THE MYTH ABOUT THE EYE

I heard they found four bees alive,
          swimming in one eye.

I heard she bathes in rose & thyme,
          instead of cloves & lye.

SPEARING STURGEON BY TORCHLIGHT

On my run, I nearly trip over a dead raccoon. I open my notes app & type, *her clouded eye.* I type, *in the poem call it a fox instead.* The neighborhood dogs haven't found it yet. This patch of skunk cabbage. These half-crushed Bud Light cans; purple beaks; lean, brackish grass. Four legs point to the gathering storm. A lifeguard whistles children out of a swimming pool. A tug with a rust-red barge churns down the East River. I watch a leaf spiral in an updraft. I watch currents braid & unbraid the thick green water.

I watch a hawk outfly the rain, just.

...

Then, rain. I think: beech, alder, ash.

I'm sitting in a window in a teal & white seersucker robe.

Waiting for an answer.

...

Estuarine. Boneless. Armored.

At dawn, men in ball caps cast lines over the railing.

I thought the dog was going to drown when it jumped off the paddleboard & my sister wouldn't let go of the leash. I thought I was going to die in the golf cart with her laughing at the wheel—hurling us over the bluff like Thelma & Louise. Sea lavender sways with the tides. We watch meteors from the dark belly of the green. In the morning, we take down the lights. Fold up the tables. Toss red & white checkered cloths in the washing machine. Stack fallen soldiers in milk crates & carry them out to the maintenance shed.

Her home is on the mainland now. But she's also here,

shucking oysters under this chestnut.

...

In the x-ray, mycelium maps a dying tree.

I think: copper to raise daffodils, foxglove to still a heart.

...

I drive back over the river. Someone hit a fox. A raven unspools the ribbon from its abdomen. A 25-foot inflatable duck bobs in the bay. An abandoned houseboat drifts closer to the island. Like the cat that came back. I hear some pennies are just bad like that.

...

I tell her I like the fire ring, the slate sink,

the beams in the kitchen she stained with tea & ink.

...

Crow eats the peanut. Cleans its beak on the deck rail. I check to see if my neighbor is watching. The rosemary is starting to yellow. I search "rosemary yellowing." On my walk, I collect mulberries in a coffee cup, smuggle somebody else's blackberries home in my t-shirt. We head north again next month. I'd like to bring her something. This fruit won't keep. Fireflies aren't here yet. The vultures are still molting in the hemlock. I find a bird's skull the size of an almond underneath the dogwood & decide to keep it.

SMALL TO MEDIUM-SIZED STREAMS

We spin in our avocado green dining room
          cute-as-a-button

catalog-built house with pocket doors garter
          snakes in the myrtle before sickness before diagnosis
before.

. . .

Dear Boy,

          I don't remember the last time

                    I picked you up,

                              Dear,   I hear this happens
                    to all parents.

          Yesterday I saw a child in the coffee shop pointing
                    at the pastry case with such fierce joy

          & wondered what's next

          for you. Too much rain or only fire.
                    Pocket green snake myrtle.

          When the news comes, you leave the tent.

                    Sit alone the mud.

          [smoke pours up
                    from the stacks across the river]

          I've said this part before, I know.

          It's just.

I want to pick you up.

Swing you on my hip.

/ Rewind

/ Rewind

/ Rewind

/ Rewind

/ Rewind

/ Rewind

. . .

King salmon steams on large tin trays. Moose meat marinates. The fiddleheads that were collected somewhere inland but marshy with oh, so many black flies four per plate / are a bit overdone / two boiled potatoes, one potato bun. The boy won't eat any of it. We walk to the Powwow grounds. Pass the charred ruins of the cathedral where his great-great-grandmother is buried. No one cares about church anymore. One daughter said midwife, the other said witch. That's what Sally said. In another time, the boy holds up an apple, touches my blonde wig / a golden dog sleeps on a hay bale / hayride / pumpkin patch / an eagle's head on a staff /

The Grand Entry has begun.

. . .

Dear Boy,

News buzzes through impossible channels.
Elder jingle grass mud.

Unimaginable to me

who carries you fleece-slung /

Snug against my body.

Bodies

keep terrible secrets,

you know.

…

I'm on the
train,

older

that
also happened.

…

Back in the village, a mom is drinking cup after cup of coffee. A toddler leaves a two-palmed smudge on the pastry case. In my dream, the boy is in college. In my dream, I am the mud of the rain-murked river, its foul gray mouth. I walk along the riverway. I stop to take a picture of a yellow & black tug chugging through the grayest nothing. A spotted lanternfly saunters along the railing / lanternfly bodies are strewn across the path. Someone carves a portrait into a pumpkin. Matt writes about floods / we all feel it.

We all feel the desolation of it.

I show him my poem.

He plays me his song.

We both know when hay rots horses go bony.

…

I'm reading about yellow blossom pearly mussels,
        presumed extinct.

We have not yet reported live or freshly dead individuals.

I cry when I see the photograph. The glass jar. Polyester.
        Red twine.

Dear Dead Water, Dear Artifact,

        Beak, beak, tooth, tooth—
                no heart, no mouth, no gill, no foot.

...

I'm reading about life-threatening rain events. About people dying in super fogs. Bowling alleys. About forest fires that burn so hot they create their own weather. Nataly says they found three bodies. Nine more are missing. The strip mining. Coal washing. Dredging. Farming. Logging. Roads. Ended them. The End. Riffle & shoal.

...

Nobody picks apples this fall. Matt & I squabble. Fruit rots under canopies swollen with rain / gurgling stink sinks into earth. This rain is relentless. Orchards reek like brown / like marsh sloshing around rushes. The train slows. A mudslide disrupts northbound service. Moss furs in violent greens across the stone's dark face.

IF YOU FIND THE STONE WALL AT THE EDGE OF THE PROPERTY

Our. Father. Son. Holy. Holy. Spirit. Word. Ochre. Cedar. Dawn.

ABANDONED PET TURTLES WREAK HAVOC IN NEW YORK CITY PONDS, GROW UNUSUALLY LARGE & KILL OFF OTHER REPTILES

Geese
paddle

through
water

thick &
algal.

It's too soon

for sun-
bathing

in piles,

too
cold

to bask

on this

log.

My mouth is a silver dollar, oh!

I swallow the baby turtles whole.

In Heaven I'll grow into it, though.

So, into the turtle pond I go.

It's beautiful out.

I'm waiting in the park to meet Vanessa for dinner.

I pry my turquoise turtle ring off my pinky finger.

Inchwide
turtles

scratch

plastic
beta fish
tanks

on 125th
Street.
Pigeons

fight for
a slice

of pizza

in a sink
hole.

Vanessa, I love this pond.

A man lifts black cloth off
a shopping cart.

Bunny or bubbles?

Spring

Dapple

Willow

Shadow

Daffodil

Star-

flower

Island.

Vanessa, I swallow the ring / the spring / the willow / the silver / the turtle / the turquoise / the tarnish / the carpet / the TV / the peach & green wallpaper / the cherries / all the juice & Sprite / the crucifix / my father's ivy / my grandfather's slippers / the box of black & white photographs in which I search for clues / the house with the sunporch & the little hill it sits below / my Easter dress / everything *else* I haven't told you about / I mean, you don't really know me yet / I swallow / the daffodils / the dapple / the shadow / the starflowers / the geese / the pigeons / the slice / 125th Street / the hole / the tanks / the algae / the log / the cloth / the bunny / the cart / the bubbles /the island /

& dive into the water.

Streetlights shudder.

Feral cats circle in Styrofoam coolers.

A jay mimics a hawk.

A man casts a line.

I got murder on my mind.

All the way down.

The hook sinks all the way down.

APOLOGY

Everyone here is day-
          drunk in the bike lane,
          dancing.

It's a street fair. Can you
          spare? I like your / a sandwich?
          jumpsuit.

Thanks,

but nothing tastes right
          anymore—

like old fish or over-
          ripe bananas.

I'm sorry I didn't love
          the way you wanted me

to love. I guess I thought
          you'd stay anyway.

I saw a five-lined skink
          this morning, sunbathing

on the mountain. Rock
          harlequins are in bloom.

SKY BURIAL

In my dream about water, I hover over a starless nothing, refusing to go in. Refusing to let tomorrow turn out like today. Sky broke. White plate. Picking porcelain out of the carpet. The phone rings. Rain churns the southwest corner of the basement into mud. In my dream about water, the waves swallow the bench I'm sitting on. I'm as small as krill. The whale's esophagus is soft & clear so there's no consequence to my being here. I collect the sunken things: cracked swim goggles, an acorn, bottlecaps, a wedding ring.

. . .

When the bird
strikes

   glass
   splinters

six diamond-

   shaped
   panes

. . .

Time is shifting. Shifts. Has shifted. Time is only. A difference. Of. Degree. Time moves differently here. It's like, when we were younger. *Now we just watch each other's faces fall,* Matt laments of middle age in these days of Zooming. I face backward on the train. Hill, river, town give way to hill, river, town. Plastic-wrapped boats & light posts. A tint of ochre on the water. Rippling. Steel. Elastic at the bridge. The embankment. Gulls cruise over the breakwater.

. . .

When I die, my mother instructs as I order her a Dunkin' decaf with almond milk, *don't put me in the ground. I won't go in a bean pot like Sharon & Dick.* No cedar clippings, silk carnations, Memorial Day set piece. No vertically planted mushroom-impregnated muslin, worms working through. Fragments of bone, cracked like oyster shells in the garden. *I want you & your sister to take me up the mountain.*

Why do you want to go up that goddamned rock? Just let the wind have me.

...

At the summit,
ravens put on
an airshow

I peel an
orange, stuff
the rind
in the pocket
of my wind-
breaker

Did you know
they can fly
for a mile
upside down?

The writer
doesn't

recognize me
later that night
in the dining
room

all cleaned
up I laugh

when she tells
me her name
again it's

burger night.

. . .

The lapsed poet forgets to tend to the Oracle's basket because her mother has been correcting her dreams again. *I had this one too.*

Glass of whiskey.

Glass of wine.

Leather couch.

Red ink.

Crossed the dream right out.

It goes like this:

I feel how hungry you are to be loved, croons the woman to the wall.

No one else sees the piebald turkey. The meadow is ringed with mist & deer. When we walk into it, we're certain we disappear. I watch a porcupine climb a tree. The lapsed poet tells me about a burial tower that's so sacred, planes must circumvent the airspace above it. *How high?* I ask. *All the way to heaven.* I send her an article about a woman who weds a 300-year-old pirate ghost. On a ship somewhere in the middle of the Atlantic, bridesmaids vomit everywhere. The captain sings: *Love is dead. Love is dead. Love is dead.*

. . .

I lose a gold earring in the gold leaves. I go running again. I go running again. I see a porcupine & think about Bridget's quillwork. *It's bad luck*, she warns, *to kill a porcupine.* Fall is porcupine season.

When Bridget sees a fresh one, she pulls the car over. My cousin jumps out. He's wearing the purple mittens Sally knitted for him. Headlights cut through fog & spray. Wipers keep a steady pulse. He spreads his raincoat over the body. Steps until the quills release.

LITTLE WITCH TUNNEL

Forget that nonsense about rhododendrons.

We walk along a root-browned river.

Alder cone. Leaf rot.

Winnie instructs me to unscrew the lid from a canning jar.

What is the meaning then.

Of ferns that blanch before browning out.

Crowsfoot. Star moss.

She points to a cluster of ghost pipes. Pale & bell faced.

Labels the jar with a Sharpie.

To be a flower is not your responsibility.

Flowers are not for superstition.

Not for guarding, Winnie says,

the entrance to the world of the dead.

ACKNOWLEDGEMENTS

Many thanks to the editors of the following publications where some of these poems (with various titles / forms) first appeared: *Allium, Ballast, Bedfellows, Best Small Fictions 2023* (Alternating Current Press), *Couplet Poetry, Grist, Heavy Feather Review, Hypertext Review, Jet Fuel Review, Mothman Was Here: Tales of the Uncanny* (Tenpenny Books), *Pidgeonholes, Tyger Quarterly* & *Wild Roof Journal.*

Research and writing of this book were supported by a NYSCA/NYFA Artist Fellowship. I'm grateful for residencies at MacDowell (where I met a lapsed poet & wrote several of the poems in this collection) & at Banff Centre for Arts and Creativity, where, on the side of Sacred Buffalo Guardian Mountain, deer helped finish this arrangement.

Dearest early readers of these poems & /or manuscript draft/s— thank you for every note. Matt Hart, I'm looking at you. Also, Gessy Alvarez, Kimberly Quiogue Andrews, Madeline Bassnett, Heather Brown, Jennifer Calkins, Marcelo Hernandez Castillo, Jessica Cuello, Quinn Franzen, Pamela Guardia, Michal "MJ" Jones, J. Vanessa Lyon, Laura Marris, Bill Neumire, Sandra Simonds, John Riccio & Alex Zipparo. If I passed you a poem across a table in a dimly lit bar, & you read it, thank you.

I have overwhelming gratitude for Jennifer Harris & the JackLeg Press team, especially Simone Muench & Lex Orgera, poets & editors extraordinaire. Thank you for guiding this book to its final form. Thank you to Anne de Marcken for knowing I would know. To the eagles, aphids, poet & moon, thank you.

Deborah Jellison, Earle Jellison, Lauren Jellison, Bridget Woodward, Ezare Millett, Melissa Farran, Kate Beschen, Karen Barone & Maria Kogan, thank you for your love, inspiration & support. To the countless family members & chosen family members not listed here, thank you.

Matt & Kit Hart. Always, always, thank you for holding my heart.

To all my ghosts, wela'lioq.

jacklegpress.org

V. Joshua Adams
Mark Baumgartner
Gayle Brandeis
Scott Shibuya Brown
Michael Chin
Chloe Clark
Rivka Clifton
Brittney Corrigan
Jessica Cuello
Barbara Cully
Allison Cundiff
Curious Theatre Branch
Neil de la Flor
Genevieve DeGuzman
Suzanne Frischkorn
Victoria Garza
Reginald Gibbons
Joachim Glage
Caroline Goodwin
Brett Hanley
Summer J. Hart
Kathryn Kruse
Brigitte Lewis
Christopher Linforth
Josh MacIvor-Andersen
Jenny Magnus
Mike McClelland
DK McCutchen
Rita Mookerjee
Mamie Morgan
Christopher Nelson
Kányin Olorunnisola
Beau O'Reilly
Lex Orgera
Zach Powers
Karen Rigby
Jo Salas
Maureen Seaton
Kristine Snodgrass
Cornelia Spelman
Peter Stenson
Melissa Studdard
Jennifer Tseng
Gemini Wahhaj
David Welch
Cassandra Whitaker
David Wesley Williams

JACKLEG PRESS

www.ingramcontent.com/pod-product-compliance
Lightning Source LLC
Chambersburg PA
CBHW030255250826
50375CB00041B/872
9781956907988